When?

When?

by

Roger Nash

First Edition

 Wet Ink Books
www.WetInkBooks.com
WetInkBooks@gmail.com

When?
by Roger Nash

Cover Design – Richard M. Grove
Layout and Design – Richard M. Grove
Cover Art – Roger Nash

Typeset in Garamond
Printed and bound in Canada
Distributed in USA and internationally by Ingram,
  – to set up an account – 1-800-937-0152

Library and Archives Canada Cataloguing in Publication

Title: When? / by Roger Nash.
Other titles: When? (Compilation)
Names: Nash, Roger, 1942- author.
Identifiers: Canadiana 20250219441 | ISBN 9781998324224 (softcover)
Subjects: LCGFT: Poetry.
Classification: LCC PS8577.A73 W44 2025 | DDC C811/.54—dc23

For Chris,
my life-long muse,
first reader and critic.

Contents

WHO'S ME?

Roger Nash

Folks sometimes ask me, "Where did you learn to write?" Creative writing at Cambridge, Toronto or Harvard? Nothing pretentious. In bed, when I was 6, and my kid brother was 3, and we shared a small bed. How could I calm his thrashing about, and perhaps get him to sleep, so I could too. I told him stories, sang him songs. I found I could do this almost endlessly, as he stayed, almost endlessly, awake – but at least quiet in the tight clasp of stories. In the end, I didn't want him – or myself– to fall asleep, as telling the stories had clasped me tight too. When I'd learned to read and write, telling stories, mainly in poems, clasped themselves into writing. And so it developed.

I write when I'm tumbled down to my knees. By wonder at the beauty of the world, and by the ambiguities, polarities and at least apparent contradictions so often present in that beauty, today. Hopes beset by tinges of hopelessness, despairs lit up by tinges of joy. We live in that kind of world in the 21st century– and was it really so different in the past – as we face the daily news. Climate-Change, no new World War but many separate wars all around the world, totalitarianism growing stronger...

I write in a kind of lyricism that's not smooth as rich verbal yoghourt – not the right lyricism for our times – but that can crackle with outrage at these ambiguities, call them out, but with a humour and patience that encourages continuing hope. Here's an example: a short poem I crafted from meeting refugee children. They sought words – as I, too, seek with them – for wonder at the might and beauty of being at sea, but in a lyricism that calls out their darkness. The poem works at empathic understanding of their vulnerabilities, as we seek to bring them back to hopes in life less beset by suspicions from their pasts.

Refugees

Refugee children, pulled ashore
after days at sea in a sinking raft.
Salt-caked words brimming
with a still buoyant lyricism of despair.
At sea, the sky had been riddled with stars.
Gulls flew by in black bruises of air.
In storms, rain fell in rubble.
Once, snow spat down.
Stumps of waves hit hard.
The days: all yellowed and crooked,
with plenty of gaps between. Thunder
coughed hard, spewed lightening
red as blood. In their still drifting eyes
hope had become a form of suspicion,
suspicion their only way to hope.

I try to write from personal experience, one way or another. I, too, have been a refugee of sorts. Growing up as a child in Egypt, civil war broke out against King Farouk. My family quickly left the village of Abu Sultan, where the mosque was burnt down, and sailed for Cyprus. There, we were housed in a refugee camp in the Troodos mountains.

Someone once said to me, "You seem to write your poems under a kind of pressure." I try to write only when I think there's something I simply have to say. I may not be sure what it is until I've said it, in the finished poem. But I'm bursting with the something I have to say. Having something to say can't be learned in a writing class. It's what you have to thrash out on your own, and then it thrashes out to be said: to call out, to learn patience and empathy for it.

Poems only have their full existence when read and heard aloud. Otherwise, they're like a song set out, perhaps so perfectly, in a musical score – that's never sung. What kind of music is that? In a poem read aloud, you can hear the trembling beat of a heart, the sound of a breathe of life. Sound mates with meaning, meaning with sound, as astonishingly and organically as animals mate in spring. The pulse and breath of a poem set the bounds of a renewed intelligibility within which we can live. Within their bounds, lives the startled or tranquil or eager heart; the breath of ecstasy, calm, terror or tears. Is life meant to be simpler, easier? No. "That's Life!" As I write, I must hear the emerging poem in at least my mind's ear, redraft it aloud, again and again, on the pulse and breath of my lips, to get its life right. My ginger cat listens encouragingly. As a co-author?

Writing poetry is a way of being aware of the world in which we live. Passionately aware! Keeping your eyes open to the humanity in everything. Keeping vital thoughts and feelings freshly alive in a freshness of language.

When?

when shadows throw people down streets
when silence bursts everyone's eardrums
when commerce stops governing the world
and sentences start with full stops

when whales catch men for their blubber
when war gains everlasting peace
when soap-bubbles sink like millstones
and ice-cubes boil the water

when fast-foods serve up democracy
when poets bankroll the treasury
when shoehorns into launch-pads grow
at that very moment or approximately

we'll reach plans to pass through
Climate Change at last at last

Hurricanes

As hurricanes track up the coast:
assault and battery, rape
and theft, by the sea. Murderously
innocent in its intimacy. Silicosis
of billows takes breath away.
Inland, no obstacles to the gales
except granny-knots of hope.
As thermometers rise, hounds
of the Baskervilles, hellcats of heat,
swoon people down;
parched fields detonate
whole crops of wheat.
Serial killing by storms:
quite legal by any laws
that govern the weather. But we manufacture
conveyor-belts of storms
ourselves, with our prolific industries.
Serial killers, we?
And murderously innocent, like the sea,
without a trace of fallible intent?
That's on a further charge-sheet.

Elegy: Forest Wildfires 2023

Hoofed forests leap,
deer race trees
with antlers flaring, birds
ignite in songs of flame,
wood-mice roar clearly,
boars hubbub
their unhewn hullabaloos,
pines fall heavy
as bent anvils, fire-breaks
wrangle and tilt their own
headstones, even cooling boulders
bleed unstaunched heat.
No ark built yet
to float on fast floods
of fire from fountainheads
of our highly molten ignorance.
Noah, too, knelled daily
on bells of black ash.

II

Porcupines on the Farm

Moonless night, black as creosote.
 I walk to the hay-barn, heavy shoulders
dragging my feet along the way.
Flashlight in pocket, just in case.
Suddenly, the night stands still,
rubbing against my leg with the farm cat
who, companionably, works the acreage for me.
I flick on the flashlight, and see her tail
stand straight up as an unbending
exclamation-mark. And, beyond that,
we're encircled by three large porcupines,
quills fully extended. History
glimmers with the focused obscurity of midnight.
A boatload of Norsemen, pikes at the ready.
Zulus defending with spears their own
right to draw breath. The abruptly
murdered come back from their pasts
to haunt my path. The porcupines rotate
slowly, like capstans of thorns, to haul
anchors or deaths from the depths of darkness.
I step back, in instant respect
for their anxiously bold and snuffling noses,
their narrow shaking shoulders. Which are mine too.
Zulus and Norsemen salute in peace.
The acreage itself owns all of us.

Of Cormorants and Us

Cormorants raise their wings to bless
the wind that dries them. Lunge after plunge
into a garotted lake of hooked beaks.
Fish spawned for execution by their thousands
of thousands in the tight noose of waters.
Last meal granted: duck-weed
and the explosion of sunlight in an airborne splash
among waves above them. No-one wears
a black cap of justice for these fingerlings.
"Well, they're only fish." Well,
we're only humans, caught in the ever-present
tyburn of peace that is war, war
that's all we know of perpetual peace.
No cap of global justice
worn for us either. Food-chains
and power-chains shape the world.
Pity-free, that's time's way
of being as fair as possible to all.
Can cormorants raise their wings to bless us?

Meeting a Wolf

I walked out in the woods one morning,
striding so fast I had to chase
my legs wherever they led: on a quest
of not knowing whatever I was fossicking for
– or whatever might be looking for me.
Then a wolf stepped onto the trail, stood still,
and stared at me. It was an old one, legs
wiry and bent as long coat-hangers
streaked with fur. It held its gaze steadily,
but with a decisive uncertainty: I just wasn't what
it was looking for, but what to hunt next?
We met each other's gaze without a blink,
finding unwavering resolve in each other's
intent uncertainty. We nodded to each other
in mutual respect of our shared ignorance.
A sudden updraft: my hat and the wolf
were gone. Whatever I sought had caught up with me:
the sheer zest of accepting the unknown every morning.

Dark Is the Best Way to Go

On far northern lakes, in winter,
dark is the only way to go.
No sunrise for weeks of rugged
twilight. We're expansively free to get lost.
Wolves howl across the bush, their coats
grey-black as each day.
For wolves, as nocturnal hunters, dusk
is entirely the best way to go.
If wolves pray, it's "Dull my Light!"
not "Enlighten my Darkness!"
And their god commanded, at the start of things,
"Let there be Gloaming outright!"
Their howl rallies the pack to hunt,
finds each other in storms,
locates clear earfuls of prey for the night.
Howls are what brighten their life-long lot.
I howl back to the wolves, discovering
our common ground. In writing poems, too,
dark is the best way to go.
Expansively free to get lost, not found,
with the sheer sound of words to lead the way.

Whale-Watching

The sea fills with underwater cathedrals.
Waves cobble their quiet naves.
Then finned arches flip tons
of black water back to front,
front to back, restless as history.
The cathedrals snort blue spray,
fill clouds with winged horses and angels.
A whirlpooled melee of our most secret desires.
Migrating, kelp-backed, to new destinations.
Tail-slapping, blunt of snout.
What desire will leap highest,
as our hearts reel in what we've never cast?
The whales — and our wildest dreams — now watching us.

Right Whales

A pod of right whales somersaults
into the bay. Their spouting eruptions
thrust up foothills, even ziggurats of sea.
The foreshore uncertain, now,
what's land or salt water.
The grassy field beneath our feet
dives deeper, with its humpbacked tons
of dandelioned tail-finned rocks.
Houses, gardens and a graveyard float
firmly on this tide, with a surging chapel
and weddings of waves. Acres of wheat
foam among their well-hedged fathoms.
We hold each other closer,
not on land or water or even in time,
as centuries thrash backwards and forwards
with huge unblinking eyes. That night,
anchors fall through the floors of our sleep.
We're sea creatures adrift on land,
land creatures walking on sea.
That's what a pod of right whales can teach us:
humans are extreme wanderers, unforgettably.

Pigeons

Three pigeons touch down on our patio.
Quite individually. One after another, then another.
As hesitantly separate as notes on an untuned
and lovelorn guitar. Tail-feathers
as blunted by wind as – being throughly modern
pigeons in a skyscraping city– skateboards
hit by labyrinths of curbs. They gather
as contestants in shyness, monitoring, with nonstop
neck-jerks, a distant closeness, a close
distance, from each other. Below, the sidewalk
gallops with shoppers, competitively maintaining,
with calibrated knee-jerks, the closest distances,
the most distant closenesses, of all.
Their glances ricochet off each other
in an everyday familiar unfamiliarity.
The pigeons abruptly concede the contest,
and leave as quickly as unanswered prayers.

With a Hound at My Heels

With a hound at my heels, time disappears.
Instead, her damp nose twitches
as steadily as the black hands of a clock.
Each moment's a now! at the crack
 of twigs under my foot: to shoot
clouds down for her to fetch.
Boulders themselves flick tails
in the well-aimed hope of her rifled sight.
With me hopelessly gun-less, her sport is hunting
the summer itself, nothing else
in view, and I'm loaded only with finishing
a poem, which she'd finish off for me,
if she could see it, in one piano-tuned
teeth-white swipe. We walk among pines
tall as stories, and crickets short
as haiku. But my hound, all senses alert
and coordinated, listens only for the sound
of the shape of the scent of the savour of deer.
Her claws grumble sharply on stones.
Still, the sun will set in a trail
of blood for her, and be there again tomorrow
for her crack-shot gunning hope.
Her wiry nerves serve the rites
of the sun. Is this the end of the poem
I was hunting for, and she's fetched it, forthright?

Opening Up the Cottage

puddles shrink
frogs' croaks
grow shorter

quilt on the line
grasshopper's chirp
airs it well

running to the outhouse
already occupied
by a pregnant fox

Hummingbird

hummingbird motionless
in fast flight
stays as it leaves
vigorous while still
hovering on an exact
pinpoint of air
beak bisecting
the petals of geometry
wings flickering
80 times
a pollened second
less than a blur
not even seen to be there
but their hum shines
in our ears the sound
of pure light

III

Steamed-Up Window

On the stove, beet-soup snores and bubbles.
A steamed-up window: the boredom of glass.
Looking out on nothing but its streaked
and dribbled self. Leaving our room
as sightless as an empty Sunday chapel.
A dripping tap stutters its drops
to rhythms of never remembered hymns.
As the steam thickens, window-frames
pull on white tight-fitting
t-shirts of water, already dripping
with sweat. Our room snoozes, waiting
for some view or another to come in
and claim it, like a stray dog at the pound,
with nowhere, but nowhere, to go on its own.
Waiting patiently to be a forever home.

Snow

When the first snow flies, instead of birds,
flowerbeds unfold fresh white
napkins, though supper's not ready yet.
A pale dough covers roofs,
goes on kneading and rising fast,
with not a bakery in sight. Footprints
in the snow outnumber walkers:
walkers overtaken by footsteps
before they get started. Lamp-posts
shrug into fluffy tight-fitting
suits, and roads become increasingly
ashen, awaiting the snow-plough's
last rites. When the phone rings
on a party-line, only a drift
of voices can try to pick it up.
A lone robin hops by, stiffly
but bravely – in red armour-plating?
Other colours scoot off, out of boredom.
Seedlings on the windowsill wait patiently,
wondering not what, but why they are.
Our constant talk about the weather: it's really
only talk about what to do with life.

A Foggy Day

No smoggy green pea-souper, this.
The fog comes in, thick and white,
from the sea. Looking out the window:
like staring into a huge bowl of soft
Basmati rice. Schools closed
because of the weather, kids run home,
popping out of the rice like screaming
chilis in their red school uniforms,
adding an essential flavour to the morning.
Lovers in parks are white-washed, at last,
into a private publicity. Houses drift
inside bleached sheeps' wool cardigans,
from chimneys to basements, all looking alike.
We walk among nothing identifiable, but all of it
strangely familiar. The untold story
of life: obfustication, opacity, invisibility
– everywhere. With everything that lacks definition
always recognizable as something else.
Cars, passing slowly, tangle fog
into pale wrap-about strings of spaghetti.

A Clear Day

A clear day, the cloudless sky
not even a metaphor for itself:
blue synopsis of a summary of zero.
Until a rainbow shivers out from nothing:
a skein of wool unrolled to knit
a many-coloured magician's sweater.
Brocaded koi swim under the bridge
of our surprise. Careful, or we'll fall in to join them.
In the zoo, bright parrots sneeze,
and return to their same unruffled position.
A rainbow is red and green and yellow
as hot peppers, it makes us both laugh and cry.
Still such a clear day, you can see
through time, both ways. Sentences have
no beginnings or endings, just this gesture
in the sky, where everything, but nothing, is said.
At least a promise that the improbable, like marriages
or wars, will go on happening – but no more
god-given floods, which we'll manufacture
ourselves by changing the world and its weather.
A gust of wind, and the rainbow vanishes,
We both slip and fall in among a slapdash of goldfish.

Shade

Shade falls from trees in the park
like waterfalls of silk. On windy days,
it sneezes in jerks on the wrinkled grass.
When the sun passes through clouds, broken
stammers on the path, trying to complete
just one sentence on what the world
is really about. On clear days,
shadows from trimmed hedges move
slowly across driveways like long sofas
on the rustiest castors. Drunks try
to sleep on them but have to crawl to keep up.
While planting new trees, a jumble-tumble
of thousands of jigsaw pieces, and some
always lost, unseen, in the nettles.
When love starts or fails, shade
reverts to fresh metaphors for what's
brand-new but well-remembered.

The Wind Has Moods

Headwinds hit you like a sack
of potatoes, bumpy all around.

Tailwinds turn peacocks'
tails into bent black umbrellas.

Updrafts steal by lifting
every ballcap or memory they can.

Downdrafts clamp on your head
like a math teacher's critical hand.

Winter squalls blow hard
as straight tots of rye whisky.

The wind knows where it's going
in its moods. Like us, a nowhere of everyplace.

IV

Lake Nepawhin

In my 82nd year, with waves praying,
and brooding sermons by an insistence of crows,
my cicada-sung house sits on a meteorite
crashsite of rocks, the sun swooning by,
salmon-red from either its Pacific
or Atlantic migrations in deep seas of sky,
the lake-front tousled with rowan-berries,
chirps, and racoons' burglary of burglar
-proof bins. Gulls shriek
as angry fishwives at their off-shore markets.
A blue heron stands on one leg,
as still as a long exclamation-mark,
waiting for its next sentence to begin.
Suddenly, with a silver flash of fish.
Nepawhin Lake is the turning world
embracing all this, from frog-spawn
to the steep truck-herding hill.
Green waves rise and fall like leaves
on trees, yet never crumble into loss
of memory, but stay as both long-term
and short-term hullaballoos of spray.
At night, moonbeams hoot with owls
for their eyes, diving on furred sleep.
At dawn, fox-tail light,
then thin porcupine needles of bright,
unveil a kingdom, queendom, creaturedom
of neighbours, finned, feathered, quilled,
leafy, hoofed or thorned, in praise
of being just perfectly alive.
A lake is a language we've never quite learned,
that tells more truths than any of our own.
My birth beats in my chest again
from 82 years ago, pulsing
with words water knows best:
I'm begotten and blessed to be here at all.
Nepawhin Lake is writing this poem
Is writing the long ripple I am.

The Small Things

When I was 12, my Mom showed me,
out on a country walk, a crater
made by a German bomb 11 years before.
The blast had blown me out of my pram then.
The crater was still stubbornly there,
but slowly filling in with dandelions,
bird-seeded saplings, small trails of silt
from spring rains. Now, in my 80's,
I try hard to believe in the small things
that'll continue to fill it: violets, barley,
a scattering of rabbit droppings, a dropped
and sorrowfully unused condom faded
forever beyond hoped-for joy,
the lost tail-feather of a bird.
Only the small things can do it.
The big things I read in the newspapers
only make more holes.
Only the small things can do it,
unobtrusively, beyond our ken or control.

An Ode to Freckles

The first girl I loved,
did she smile broadly over her freckles,
or freckle widely over her smile?
In political protests, those freckles
heckled more loudly than most.
At restaurants, her cheeks had all
the salt and paper at each table.
She was everything I savoured for weeks.
Her face was the whole world,
even alternate worlds, to me.
In spring, her forehead hazy
as fields we walked in. In summer,
dappled as shade we sat in
under a tree. By a stream, every
fleck speckled. In a car,
more studded than its spinning wheels.
After her visits to dermatologists,
my whole world, the alternate
worlds too, were, blankly, lost to me.
Did she marry an accountant?

Out of Nowhere

Singleton Park, Swansea

She came out of nowhere, the best
place for future wives to come from.

She taught me that nowhere isn't a vacuum,
but a park full of magnolias in bloom,

and cocker-spaniels walking their owners.
The gates get locked at sundown.

Skate-Marks

An amazement of mazes: our sons carve
pond ice with the high speed
of laughter. Spin themselves lost to the world.
To find, by skedaddling over snow-banks,
untrodden future lives. Glancing
back with a joyful lack of nostalgia.

Or are the mazes a labyrinth? Under the ice,
a Minotaur tries to rise, searching
for cracks. Waiting, his mouth full
of water, for heroes to re-sharpen
their skills and jump over his rippling back
– as is respectfully due by ancient tradition.

As blades wear blunt, kids
skate slower, shout faster.
That's communication on a rink.
Unless skate-marks are long scrawls,
in scraped dictionaries of strange alphabets,
where kids scornfully explain to their parents:

"Looking back aint no good
for grownups neider." In each switchback
script, a last flourish, firm
and thin as bones in the blackbird's song:
"World's bigger than 'tis, because we'm smaller
than we am. No skul today."

An Oriental Carpet

We step out of bed each morning and stand,
perfectly still, on the carpet, but moving everywhere,
as it lies actively inert on the floor.
A woven kaleidoscope of sweeping forms.
Fish and clouds, burrows and birds,
deserts and fruit, darkness and flowers.
Threaded together at our feet, we with them.
A fine-spun genesis for words and deeds,
truths or skulduggery, for the rest of the day.
As the world unravels in the hourly news,
the rug will knot everything back together,
us too, for the start of tomorrow. To begin, again.
On a floor full of hoofed forests.
And no seas as deep or shallow,
sailed or unsailed, as the one we're standing on.

Long Walks

Long walks are good for your health.
But I need an important destination
to get me out each day to do them.
The same destination wherever I go.
I'm on my way to touch an apple
my mother left on the table before
I was born. My walk is always a huge
success. However far I go,
the apple and its table are always a bit
further on, so I can walk and then walk and then walk.

Rebel!

Rebel against the cancered skin you can't live within.
Revolt against the tyranny of daylight and dark.
Riot against the pinpoints of the starry night.
Defy the kingship of the forceful sea.
Mutiny against the parliaments of rain and drought.
Mock the faulty leadership of both heart and head.
Flout the autocracies of love and hate.
Declare war against whatever destiny is.
Accept only the song of the robin on the lawn.
For it can sing within whatever it sings within.
Accept the first crocuses of spring.

My Street Corner

The corner of my street: so curvingly-straight, its shape
can't be named by geometry, after a century
of the city's creative re-planning. Only its shape
can describe its shape, wordlessly, in a stutter that's locked
forever within a lip-reading paper-cut tongue.
No words for this corner can straighten it out
in an exact and plainly literal route of telling.
Only switchbacks of analogies and parables will do,
for a sense of place that's not literally, but is really, true.

The shape of the corner in my street is gingerly blue,
where wind sticks a pizza'd tongue in your mouth,
rain falls like drum-majors on parade,
and clouds bump and preen each other
as much as bored baboons. Early gardens
here are still and empty as flat balloons.
Trees beside it grow as stiffly as Stalin
but dance like Charlie Chaplin in a strong blow.
Ambulances brake and stop at this bend constantly:
no-one to bring back again from the morgue.
Schoolgirls wait on it with dyed hair (the years
are blonder than they were), wearing noses and fingers
under rings they seem to have been born with.
That's the corner of my street for you, part of a world
full of flukes and haphazards, not straight and literal.
Not a corner at all, but a ladder up
to seeing things always further and differently.
And if you think too much, you're not thinking at all.

Falling in the Bath

This morning, she fell in the bath. Random,
not everyday, but, inevitably, more often.

Like being a child again, waking up suddenly
in a dark room and wanting her so-recent dream back.
Crying because she can't remember what it was,
but still demanding it back, of necessity,
as it quite freely came and went.

Being a child again, at 85,
is six of one and a half dozen of the other.
You're free to pick, but it's unavoidable to do it.
Like distinguishing dalmatians: more dog, less spot.

Yesterday, she couldn't remember the name of the street
where we live. More dog, less spot, both bite.
For her, the last straw that broke the "whatsit's?" back.

She remembers her mother mending and re-dressing
a doll she broke. But was it the same doll?
Did she love it still, or want the old one back?
A half dozen eggs seems better than six.

V

Tides

Around the world, nation after nation achieves
mass murder in the name of freedom,
raises democracy to the dragging of chains.
Each minute of each day,
a turning of the tides that run through our lives:
hopes rushing in while they're drawing out,
oppositions and turbulence everywhere.
Our dreams, though as long-enduring as pebbles,
just roll this way and that.
We're caught in the intestines of an invisible sea
that swallows us while retching us fully up.
Our plans for the future have the zest of a billow,
roller, breaker, surf, spume,
then bright whitecap. Then the same in reverse.
We must learn to swim the rip-tides in our hearts.

Catching Up with the News

Ukraine, Gaza...

These days, we can't watch the news: clods
of children piled beside skyscraping rubble.
Pianos played by hammers and hacksaws.
War is like gravity: it enfolds us everywhere.
Peacemakers push hard as snowploughs
in heatwaves. To have a body at all,
as it bleeds to death: as indescribable and unnatural
as G-d. Wars start, throughout history,
because "Never again" means "Let's try again
in our next orgy of self-glorifying self-hate."
Saints, in all our places of worship,
wear halos of brightly-lit hornets.
Each poem is a headstone for itself.

The Power of Balconies

In Kyiv, on a bombed building,
a loyal balcony tilts.
Lines of defiant washing
dry across it. But a Romeo
below could still try
to sing to a Juliet above.
Even a blessing could be uttered from it,
to a whole world, no less,
urbi et orbi, after a conclave
of peace-makers has met.
As a balcony, it's a place that patiently
awaits some ceremony or another
– as balconies must. True enough,
a small boy runs out
and gets his head stuck
between its railings. The ceremony of playing
among ruins as one grows up.

The Pregnancy-Test Quiz

After a clear and wonderful test result,
the unanswered questions start. Boy or girl?
With wings at its heels or cloven hoofs?
Or an Achilles' tendon of aching truth?
Will s/he live life on a reel that cameras
shot, the sun an arclamp of bright?
Scenes missed or cut or dropped
in mud? Will s/he kiss warm celluloid,
or many pairs of eager lips?
Be lost in a leaning tower of words
or quite able to see horizons waving
their verbs? Will s/he walk towards love
more slowly than a tortoise in a broken
hearse? Find joy often as heavy
as macadam, sadness as light as dust?
Can we answer these questions with other tests?

Luggage for the Paddle-Wheeler

Suitcases ripple
in their alligator hides.
Ready to swim
if the cruise-ship sinks.
Backpacks snarl
zippers like incisors.
Ready to chew rivals
for a place at the bar.
And the travel agent
talks on, nonstop,
to enhance the improbable.

Having a Shower

She wears her shower as a dress-parade:
hair effervescing in ripples of sequins;
a cascading scarf of words at her mouth;
her gown, as tight as a spill of silk,
swirled first on one, and then the other,
and then on both entirely flowing shoulders;
a sudden but unstoppable cloudburst of breasts;
both legs slimly spangled
with seams as rainbowed as soap-bubbles;
a well-sewn hem of foam
around the eddying surge of her gurgling toes.
She steps from the shower as a tall clothes-horse
to dry every wardrobe of water.

Tears

In Obstetrics, a mother drenches with tears
of splendor. Just before, they deluged with effort.
Same tears, but do they know they're different?
After school exams, light dew
 or a regular hosing in the eyes of students.
Who passed, who failed?
Streaks on faces can't tell.
At a wedding, both bride and groom
sprinkle, wet faced, at the camera.
At a divorce, both sprinkling again.
Which spray says coming together,
which drizzle, tumbling apart? Weathers
and tear-glands stay ambiguous.
More bliss at falling apart?

Hiccups

A hiccup is a set-up
by the g-god of bad occasions.
At the start of an acceptance speech,
it shouts the rudest limerick.
A private kiss: as public
as an unpinned mouth-grenade.
Excommunicated by speech.
Jettisoned overboard down
the waves of your own throat.
A loud fart from your mouth,
a belch from both ears.
On the bright side, welcome them
for their firm stand on gender
rights: women and men
assigned them quite equally.
And in our space-age, they can spin you
around like the fastest sput-hik.
Best of all, in art-shows,
they recreate us in parts, above
and below the diaphragm, then a head
on top: a human triptych-hik
to hang, crooked, on the wall.

Whispers

A whisper is a dead man's shout,
or a neonate's hungry cry. Too soft
to tell which is which. Or is it both?
It's a cat's whisker brushing your ear.
A whisper is the cork on a full bottle
of dangerously over-proofed voice.
Whispers: thick rubber soles
on a long-distance running commentary.
A whisper is well-gated breath,
but a bull the other side of the fence.
It's bridling your tongue while the horse still jumps.
A whisper is quiet as a sunbeam in the air,
or sinks to the floor like a deflating balloon.
In an age of technology, it's sound-proofed ridicule.
It's an aside to G-d, so S/He won't hear it,
or an atheist's decorous disagreement with Fate.
A whisper is truth stuck in your throat.

After all the whispers, silence falls
 on the room like a sackful of goose-feathers,
floating everywhere, clinging to your coat.

A Yacht

Moored hard to the dock, her sail
stretched tight-lipped, counting
every cormorant flying by.
Earnestly billowing each perfume
out of the sky. Blueberries
and drying hay. At eager rendevous
for anything to happen. Her own tiller-hand
for anywhere the wind will go. Will go.
Ship-shape, but not for bobbing,
port-worthy, among sherry parties.
Ship-shape for something imperative
in her perfection. Sheer energy carved
in her bow like a swooping sea-hawk.
As the wife she's named after, "The Abigail"
slipped free from her port, and left
a would be human owner. Unmanned.
In full sail. To whatever happened.

A Kiss

Among the huge ambiguities of language: lips
at their most ambiguous while saying nothing
at all. In quick kisses at the hectic airport,
we greet and we part, one kiss
much like another, welcoming our farewells.

Then when Eric gave Kent
the kiss of life, after his stroke in the street,
he knew they'd stay as opposed as ever
over where lot-lines should be.
Re-starting a pulse to be angry together.

Girl's first kisses, in a boyfriend's
sports-car, roughed by the tread-marks
of a speed-breaking beard. She'd rather
walk for the rest of her life than be run over
by puckered pairs of brake-free lips.

A man's shy and last peck
on the nose of his dying wife. Shy,
because he's not used to her being dead.
Last, but just like the peck he gave her
on their first date a lifetime ago:

a kiss with everything, ambiguously, still
before them, death-bed or not.

Sticks

Great-grandfathers walk in the park
every summer, tapping hard
dry earth with their walking sticks.
Dab, rap, clip, clump.
Great-grandfathers change year
by year, but the sticks stay the same,
in the cycle of life. On rocks, a clout
like hooves of wild goats from the most ancient
of times. The men focus on following
their sticks, wherever alpenstocks are alert
to go. They don't talk to one another
but listen intently to the pulse in their ears
of each other's thumping canes.
The pulse never dies out,
an intimation of immortality in the park.
Thud, thwack, knock and jab.
They raise their sticks occasionally, to point
at the sky. Will it rain tomorrow?
The immortality of doubt – and hope.
As the sun sets, they aim at the great
hooded owl of the rising moon.
As if drawing a bead on it made it come about.
As if the moon is what they're walking towards,
striving for, promise themselves, aspire to,
will soon – if not already – have taken up.

Nikos Solomos at Ninety-Five

A small rowboat scuds around his bay
each night. But no-one else can see it.
He wonders: can Charon work even
in Canada? On special visas? Coming
to ferry him off? In his 95th year
of the ambiguities in life, he takes a coin
from his wallet. In an uncertain just-in-case.
To pay the Ferryman. As tradition dictates.
No Greek coins, but a Quarter,
Canadian, must do. Then he sticks it back.
Surely it's already well organized
by Some Committee, Some Where,
Some Time, Some What:
he can exceed his due limits, genetic
or whatever they be. With a surplus of Wars
and Climate-Change and Covid, there's an excess
of unlived life to use up. So he'll negotiate
with Destiny as riddle-me-ree as anyone likes.

She

She strode like a dancer.
Swam like swans flying.
Floated like a lotus.
Slept like small geraniums.
Awoke busy as a highway.
Cussed like rusty brakes.
But sang like a pizza.
Her ideas always handy
as Swiss Army knives.
She smiled like hot treacle.
Could jump like a "Bingo!"
But dropped like a stone.

VI

Reversals

factory farming
a strutting light switches on
the rooster crows hard

our dog brings me rocks
because I won't shoot ducks down
the rocks fold their wings

butterflies float past
like parasols of petals
and even give shade

a fly buzzes hard
in a cleanly washed jamjar
is he lost, or me?

when you lose at cards
storms shuffle by overhead
deal the sky again

A Medley

i
On a tin roof, rain gallops
like horses, nonstop. Until you know
it's really horses galloping like rain.

ii
Copy-editing: commas swarm
on a page like black sperm, desperately
seeking a single ovum of thought.

iii
Conquerors salt or land-mine the land.
Nothing grows but tears. Nothing
walks but legless hands.

Nightly Migration of Geese

Over the insomnia of the sea, church bells,
hammered by a gale, alert the geese
to keep flying south all night.
Mountains step sideways in the dark,
to encourage them. The birds' eyes close
on our landscapes. They focus only on the minarets
of stars. Their blood pumps in the wings
of their dreams, as does ours, as we dream,
stockstill in bed, of our migrating,
ever-shifting, unplanned destinies.

Moving House Too Often

A tap is dripping slowly, somewhere.
Can't find a leak anywhere.
Must be dripping at our previous address.

Our new keys won't turn in the lock.
Perhaps they only open a door
to our next house after that.

When, with sheer nostalgia, I ring the bell
in our old residence, lights go on
– or fuse – in our new one instead.

Our wrinkled mail arrives regularly,
but bills are redirected to someone
we haven't quite become yet.

When I dig snow from our driveway,
it only piles thicker. Unless
I'm shoveling our last place by proxy.

A dog barks all night.
Either the jackal of our well-gnawed dreams,
or in the back porch of a future habitat.

Still, we water each garden consistently.
"Snapdragon." "Sweet William." "Forget-me-not."
The names we live in are a lasting home.

Progress

Progress is irresistible, relentless, majestic, a crook.
We're schooled in yoga, aerobics, calisthenics and hand-guns.
More roads for more cars: coffin-lids for farming.
Born horsemen drive by who'll never see
– unless they eat it in a restaurant – a free-ranging horse.
Fast foods go faster: pizzas
as meteorites of yet untasted light.
Candies grow even sweeter in their sky-blue
cloudless cartons, rattling with well-shared obesity.
Though we split atoms easily, split selves
find it harder and ever darker to unite.
You advance further than me, them
than us, proliferating our freely-given inequality.
Sex unfolds without boundaries, but we're tangled
in uncertainties which genders to enact or discard:
she's both, he's neither, they're...
Finished. And money never misses a chance
to show the status quo of stupidity.

Technology

Technology, too, is a part of nature,
with nothing in nature untouched by us.
Stars twinkle while recharging their batteries.
Meteors fly by as unguided drones.
Farmers fell forests to pasture
interbred herds of snorting burgers.
Boulders sing at a pitch below hearing,
and their records will top all the charts.
Kids chisel wings off flies,
but flies equalize with wingless viruses.
Chimps claim human descent.
We'll settle out of court on that.

How Many?

How many wars
has our shared nuclear threat
deterred? Will we ever know,
since they never occurred?
Yet those who plan this threat
see deflected wars as part
of the real world they must prepare for.
It's like deaths parried, world-wide,
by Covid vaccines, where last
gasps have never – yet – been drawn.
Though medical statistics hear
and quietly record them. To be fair,
this world of the provisionally actual
– or is it the actually provisional? –
strives to keep an uncertain
balance between the good and the bad.
The many marriages that would've lasted
had breathless marriage promises
been kept? "We can give you figures
on that." These marriages will endure
for eternity, because nothing can break
provisional love-making up.
But likewise, the wars we held off
can never really end.
How do you sign a truce
with the Provisionals' brigade of bayonets?
Between the good and the bad, can we hope
for more than a provisional draw?

The Age-Old "Canon of Poetry": Can It Reach Our New Times?

Dear Reader, if that's you, watch
for the Green Knight or Piers Plowman,
 or the Wife of Bath, to see what they're doin'.
They're only me, or you, in our long
and historic yen to be others: the trickiest
yen to watch of all. Will they slip,
in a land new to them (how did the Wife
ever get past Canadian Customs?),
on our northern snowdrifts of white paper?
When snow can't type at all,
and buries quill pens. Will they be able
to stand up again, as so much
white paper has fallen, a record
this year? Can we hoist them up without renting
a high crane of internet telephones,
the biggest there is? The Wife of Bath,
or is it me or you? (I think it's you, nearly)
now manages a top women's
soccer team, whose games score
new words; the Knight talks
his head off as a truth-telling rapper;
and Piers still ploughs fields,
sitting in a million dollar tractor
of AI generated poetry,
which can do anything you want, even
before you ever, yet, wanted it to.

Time

In conversation with Auden

"Will the plant in this pot grow?" Time
will tell. "Will she love me or not?" Time
will tell, and hasn't told him anything yet.
But perhaps the question is wrong for time
to answer, with just those two alternatives.
She both loves him and not, alternately;
or constantly, in a perfectly settled and loyal
state in-between. "When will time
disclose all the things it has to tell us?"
A question on the minds of stock-market investors.
Or is time's telling anything just a fib
spread by the elderly, to seem wise as well as old?
Time will reveal that too.
Perhaps time already answered, long ago,
but to someone other than the questioners: a man
sprawled in a bar, or a weeping toddler.
Maybe divulged yesterday, but in Old High
German, a language no one still speaks.
Plausibly, its time that polarizes the world
in our mutual ignorances. But only time can tell.
And, in all of history, it's not confided, yet.

Ode to Dust

In the dust you stand in, wherever you are,
great cities have been sacked and fallen,
new loves begun, children born
under hedges, another Messiah proclaimed
and then flung into clink. Wherever you walk,
in city squares or dense forests,
the dust is full of forgotten footprints,
dragging or skipping their heels. Whatever
vacuum-cleaner adverts say,
it's not to be loudly condemned and quickly
swept or sucked away. Instead,
raise a quiet and respectful salute.
For in silt or sand is the length of our history.

Size

The Lord's prayer, written on a grain of rice.
Love your neighbour but grow a tall hedge.
Salvation's bottle is always too small.
Children's tears, twice the size of their eyes.
Just beyond reach, the biggest blackberries of all.
Skinny horses have the fattest clouds of flies.
The tinier the detail, the chunkier the devil that's in it.
With sales of kingsize homes, houses show their owners.
The ground either too high or low
for newborn lambs with four jello'd legs.
Even on the worst of days, everything's still
in its place, if we know where to put it.
The girth of the Big Bang, that started everything,
if measured with a carpenter's tape, nothing at all.
Asking the most difficult questions makes
hunchbacks of the straightest of straight lines.
Top rungs of ladders – for ever the wrong height.
A camel's eye can pass though the eye
of a needle, to reach both our births and shrouds.
Size is all metaphor, whatever its measurements.

Stop-Lights

Stop-lights
stuck on red.
No sugar for coffee.
A missile off course.
A peace not made.
A war not properly declared.
A promise not kept.
A death in the family.
A promise not made.
An unfaithful lover.
An earthquake not predicted
by astrologers, astronomers
or even Aunt Mary.
Stuck lights
back up a trend
for the whole world
at a single rush-hour.

Vancouver's North Shore Mountains

The endless life of the North Shore
Mountains: wiped out each morning
by the perhaps perpetual life of thick
sea mist. When that shifts, the mountains
are reborn, post-latte, but not looking
quite exactly the same. More Zelenskys
of altitude not as much Alexanders as before.
Or in hard rain, Hitlers rather than Caligulas
of landslides, and roped, slippery, rescues.
Mountains mount atop other mountains,
as peoples rise atop other peoples,
their lives bemisted, in each morning's
newscast, by the unending return of perhaps
well-intentioned, but indelibly final,
wars. Can we go on sipping our apparently
uncountable lattes, with another David
or Ibrahim, Rebecca or Rabeeah, born
and then disappearing, cyclically, just as before?
North Shore Mountains come and go
in the mist, with the dark silhouettes of centuries.
As much our collective history, as mountains at all.

At Around Midnight

At around midnight, the silence that stuffed
our ears with cotton-wool, fell out
with a clang on our goose-down pillows.
At about midnight, fire-trucks
pranged cop-cars in the middle
of highways, and ambulances started fires
with their soaring sirens. At close to midnight,
orthodox believers rolled over into being
the strictest atheists, and atheists rolled over
and fell out of bed onto faithful carpets.
Lovers felt suddenly lonely, and the lonely
dreamed of a bed of endless lovers.
Children turned into the adults they'd hoped
they'd never have to be, and adults
cried for their great-great-grandmothers.
The living woke up to be almost dead,
but the dead had almost enough sleep to last
for around, about, or close to, forever.

Ode to All the Nowheres

Out of nowhere, nowhere hits you head on.
Cars aren't built to take nowheres like that.
"You immigrants came out of nowhere."
"We're out of nowhere but just where we are."
Debts pile up out of nowhere.
Bills from places never heard of.
Marriages thrive or break out of nowhere.
Lots of nowhere in a king-sized bed.
Out of nowhere? Shortest distance of all.

Tree

I listened to a tree speak to me in May.
I couldn't understand a breath of it, but listened anyway.
Sometimes it sang, a song without a singer,
a song without words, each leaf
flickering its own green grammar.
What it whispered: the gift of being windily alive
without a thought in my rustling head.
Not sure I was there as more than a tree myself.
Just listening to the trees. Part of a forest,
without a cogito ergo sum under my scalp.
The air so clear, I wasn't sure I was there at all,
or had always been there, or would take root tomorrow.
Each leaf lisped separately,
but also as part of a unified choir,
forever well-rehearsed without a conductor.
I listened to a tree one May, its song
and May still always around me. We sing
to the perfect but unconducted order of the cosmos.

A Fig Tree

The wind gusts in from the sea, whistling
across our verandah. Can my fig tree, frisking
in its large pot, entice the wind
to keep blowing, keep blowing?
As leaves samba swaying skirts,
can it charm the city's high-rises
to loosen their tightly trendy architecture,
swivelling to face her with goggling windows
ensnared? And can the scent of black figs
– coddled in wine, cloves and peppercorn –
pack the streets, leaving no room
for cars to steer toward a day in the office
beside the bumper-to-bumper bewitchments of summer?
As she jigs taller into her green rigging
of air, can she flirt with a thousand ships
in the harbour riding on a thousand-and-one waves,
so they sail to shores not ruled by "the Economy"?
She tempts, allures, then startles away all
the giddy pigeons, to unfold her own
jade wings, so the whole city
can fly. Her leaves swirl on the borders
of the deepest dreams. In which a fig tree
might redeem the world – since we cannot.

VII

Dreams in a Heat-Wave

On our nights of record temperatures, pillows
gum down like unopened envelopes.
But were there any dreams inside them at all,
or just tossing about half-awake?
I try to interpret a dream in the middle
of a dream, but only dream I'm asleep.
Over 40 degrees tonight, and cluttered
with only half-asleep dreams that're like...
recycled spam in an email account:
we owe money in a mortgage we don't own,
inherit fortunes from relatives we don't have.
After reading a few, delete the lot.
When their internet goes down, we'll wake up.
Modeh Ani* and eye-rubbing
hopefulness: a better start
to the day than dreams that AI wrote
by the alert, as always, algorithms of chance.

Hebrew: I thank you. Opening words of traditional Jewish prayer upon waking.

Short-Staffed Post-Covid

Today is away when you go to the clinic.
It'll be back in a year. There are now
just 9 months in a year,
as months are badly understaffed.
We need to hire more from countries
with plenty of well-qualified Novembers.
The sun will rise every second
day, as supply-lines for astronomy
are badly broken. Thursday resigned
from the week as continually overworked.
It's out fishing all the time,
threatening rainbow-trout and appointments
with extinction. And, of course, the 10th man
for a minyan* will still always be lacking.
Some important shortages stay enduringly
stable. So stop complaining, why not.

* Heb: quorum for prayer.

A Story of Mizrach* in my Town

"My heart is in the East, and I in the uttermost West." (Yehuda ha-Levi)

In the late 1800's, it was.
Pioneers camped in the forest where, later,
my town would be built. To prospect
for laying down a Pacific railway line.
But needles in their compasses spun every
which way. They couldn't map where
they were. And the lake they found just shouldn't
be there. So they called it "Lost Lake" –
as indeed they were. A cobbler and cook
didn't know which direction
to face in prayer. Did Lost Lake,
make them Lost Jews? Was Jerusalem,
itself, Lost Jerusalem from here?
Then the words of Yehuda ha-Levi
came to them, from the eleventh century in Spain:
"My heart is in the East." Whichever way
they faced, as they prayed in snow or rain,
dark clouds filling the sky,
they prayed in the direction of their hearts, in vows
and thankfulness. Afterwards, nickel deposits
– magnetic – were detected in rocks around the lake.
Very dizzying for magnetic compasses.
But for a cook and a cobbler, Lost Lake
and two Lost Jews were already
securely found, even if needles
of compasses spun endlessly around.

Heb: the East.

70

A Wall in Poland

The wall has as many bullet-holes as bricks.
Built of executions barely held together
by ageing cement. Never again.
"And never even this first time."
Hope tries to expand to that:
to grasp their hands, dragging them back
before they're shot. But our memories have flaming
swords in hand, to bar us from leaping through them,
as gateways, to change the bullets' marks.
Yet a blessing can go where memory cannot,
striding into the past to grasp, for us, the hearts
of those lined up against the wall.
"Baruch dayan ha-emet:"*
"Blessed be Thee, True Judge."
We bless a great unfolding of history
– in the face of the evil as well as the good –
towards greater justice and truth.
Then those shot at the wall will have died,
in our blessing, in a forever unslaughtered struggle
for peace in future lives as thronged
as grains of sand with children's laughter.
Memory cannot save their lives,
but it is up to us to save their struggle.
Then the wall is built of an enduring quest
for the future as much as bricks with bullet-holes.

*Heb: blessing offered, traditionally, when faced with a tragic loss of life.

Best-By

"Most devious is the heart; It is perverse — who can fathom it?" (Jeremiah 17.9)

Millions of dead, wounded, refugees,
in current wars around the world.
Has the Bible reached its best-by date?
To be put out with the stale bread,
the rusty and tinseled crucifixes,
any mouldering manna still left about,
the dented cans of mushroom soup?
Politicians speak with lying lucidity.
Soldiers speak with the opaqueness of truth.
Is that blood on G-d's biblical face?
Will S/He smile on us with another best-by Face?
Another stack of freshly-baked ordinances?
Or is that final and unredeemable best-by date
only for the pell-mell dark our own hearts have reached,
as we hurl ourselves into our global tip?

Hunger

Palavering hubbubs of mallards on the lake.
Demanding their inalienable right to eat
duckweed. A heron stands on the steadfast
steeple of one leg, praying silently
– and mercilessly – for fish. A child in a dumpster
digs for the corrugated cardboard of pizza.
Hunger, like love, never gives up.
Armies march on their stomachs, stomachs
trample their armies down. Trample
even languages too, until a torn page
of fish-and-chips stained newspaper
tastes more deeply meaningful
than words to the kid in that cold dumpster.
For what words could say, more clearly than that,
that millions of kids, in war or peace,
are starving and weren't fed today.
As weighty as all other commandments combined:*
"Give food to the hungry and poor."

* See Talmud, Bava Batra 9a:12.

Mazal Tov!*

What happens to us by mazal or luck,
is as though decreed by the most distant stars.
Conversational constellations no less,
speaking nonstop in the much-attended
zodiac columns of the daily news.
Yet it's proclaimed, by a proverb in Ladino lands,
"To change your village is to change your mazal."
Then how we, ourselves, choose to journey
through life, lobs the stars themselves
into our hands: we shape their twinkles on our days.

It happens I first met my wife-to-be
– such good luck! – in a train station,
when I could've stayed at home instead.
Mazal greeted my future love and I
not up in a distant sky,
 but right there on platform three.
Let's sing Mazal tov! to others
more frequently, its providence a kind of organized
uncertainty in our travels through time, whatever
the number of our train's platform may be.

*Heb: literally, good luck; colloquially, Congratulations! Also denotes, in its
history, a sign of the zodiac.

Stolperstein*

Walking down a side-street in Cologne,
my wife and I suddenly trip
on an unnoticed *stolperstein*. Our hands
shoot out sideways to find other
hands to steady us. But our fingers grasp
only silent thin air in an empty street.
We grasp for the ungraspable absence
of – looking down at a brass plate
on the cobblestones – Martha and Baruch.
We've stumbled into, not onto their lives.
No longer a statistic, they live
in this very house, our neighbours on the street.
At this very front door.
                        How can we change
a world so full of empty embraces,
hand-grasps on thin air?
My wife and I hold hands,
tightly and earnestly: the way towards an answer,
for us, for now. We thank you, our neighbours
Martha and Baruch, for showing us that.
These stumbles of enlightenment aren't something
you can bypass, like the City Museum. Stumbles
just happen, wherever you are.
Memory is decentralized, on thousands of streets,
where *stolpersteine* shine by rows of doors.

*German: stumble-stone; plural stolpersteine. Concrete cube bearing a brass
plate with the name, life-dates, date of deportation or massacre, of a victim
of Nazi extermination. Placed at the last place they lived, worked or studied.*

Torah

The Torah is rarer by far than radium,
but as ever-present as your very next breath.
It rouses us to calm through its safe unrest.
Despite digital clocks, the Torah
keeps not Greenwich, but Moses mean-time.
It shouts loudly into the waxed silence
of our ears, whispers in hubbubs
of the flag-waving protests of crowds.
It speaks on your i-phone when you don't answer it:
no message, but call back, please.
In prisons, it encourages handcuffed hopes.
Its voice is heard even on satellites
and under eel-weaving seas.
It hails all nations on loudspeakers
of pooling tears. When the soup-pot
is nearly empty, the Torah is packed
with herrings in schools of words. In Torah
even the dust shall sing, and wheat
sprout in deserts of the driest hearts.
When you chant it in minyans, there's no you
and me, only the self-of-the-minyan,
assembled continuously on its buoyant tongue.
Living in the history of "we," not "me".

About the Author

Roger Nash is a past-President of the League of Canadian Poets, and inaugural Poet Laureate of Sudbury. As President of the League, he worked with Senator Grafstein to create the Parliamentary Canadian Poet Laureate position in Ottawa. He's published twenty-two books of poetry, short fiction and philosophy.

Literary awards include: the Canadian Jewish Book Award for Poetry, the PEN/O.Henry Prize Story Award, the Confederation Poets Award (twice), and first prizes in poetry contests with *Prism international* and *The Fiddlehead*.

Roger was born in the blitz in England, and grew up in Egypt and Singapore. He came to Canada in 1965, living mainly in Sudbury, but also in Guelph, Edmonton and Vancouver. He's Professor Emeritus in Philosophy (environmental ethics) at Laurentian University, and a Fellow of Thorneloe University.

Also by Roger Nash

Poetry
Settlement in a School of Whales
Psalms from the Suburbs
Night Flying
In the Kosher Chow Mein Restaurant
Once I Was a Wheelbarrow
Uncivilizing
Something Blue and Flying Upwards: New and Selected Poems
The Sound of Sunlight
Upsidoon
Zigzags
Whazzat?
Climbing a Question
The Pollen of Strange Alphabets
World of Difference

Fiction
The Camera and the Cobra and Other Stories

Editions
Spring-Fever
Licking Honey off a Thorn
Northen Prospects: An Anthology of Northeastern Ontario Poetry
Our Lakes Shall Set Us Free

Philosophy
Ethics, Science, Technology and the Environment:
Reader and Study Guide
The Poetry of Prayer (second expanded edition)